WITHDRAWN

Written
by
Stuart A. Kallen

Published by Abdo & Daughters, 4940 Viking Dr., Suite 622, Edina, Minnesota 55435.

Library bound edition distributed by Rockbottom Books, Pentagon Tower, P.O. Box 36036, Minneapolis, Minnesota 55435.

Copyright©1993 by Abdo Consulting Group, Inc., Pentagon Tower, P.O. Box 36036, Minneapolis, Minnesota 55435. International copyrights reserved in all countries. No part of this book may be reproduced without written permission form the copyright holder. Printed in the U.S.A.

Edited by Julie Berg

Cover photograph: by Vic Orenstein
Interior photographs: by Vic Orenstein
Special thanks to: The Target Earth™ Kids–Jennie, Libby, Joe, Ted, Kenny & Grace
Artistic Consultant: Patti Marlene Boekhoff

Library of Congress Cataloging-in-Publication data

Kallen, Stuart A., 1955-
    Eco-games / written by Stuart A. Kallen.
      p.   cm. -- (Target Earth)
    Includes bibliographical references.
    Summary: Provides instructions for making and playing games spotlighting environmental protection, recycling, and ecology.
    ISBN 1-56239-201-8
    1. Environmental education--Activity programs--Juvenile literature. 2. Ecology--Juvenile literature. 3. Recycling (waste, etc.)--Juvenile literature. [1. Ecology 2. Recycling (waste) 3. Games. 4. Handicraft.] I. Title. II. Series.
GE77.K35   1993
    363.7--dc20   93-7750
                                                                                               CIP
                                                                                               AC

The Target Earth™ Earthmobile Scientific Advisory Board:

Joseph Breunig–Curriculum Integration Specialist at the Breck School, Minneapolis.
Beth Passi–Education Specialist; Director of the Blake Lower School, Minneapolis.
Joseph Reymann–Chairman of the Science Department at St. Thomas Academy, St. Paul.
Larry Wade–Scientist-in-Residence for the Hennepin County School District, Minneapolis.

 Thanks To The Trees From Which This Recycled Paper Was First Made

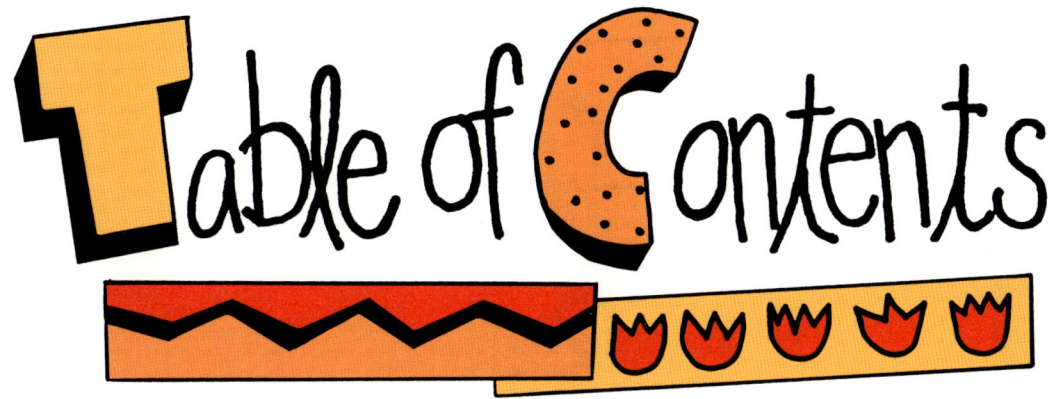

Let's Begin Here 4
Chapter 1 - Indoor Eco-Fun **5**
Eco-Jigsaw Puzzle 5
20 Questions Eco-Board Game.. 7
Eco-Cards 9
Eco-Quiz 13
Chapter 2 - Outdoor Eco-Games **16**
Sock Pop 16
Slippin' and Slidin' 18
Do the Can Can 19
Eco-Scavenger Hunt 21
Chapter 3 - Serious Fun **23**
The Garbage Game 23
Adopt A Park 26
Answers to Eco-Quiz 30
Connect With Books 31

Let's Begin Here.

Global warming, animal extinction, and pollution are pretty serious problems. Luckily for us, there are some pretty serious people working to solve those problems. But if anything is going to change, everyone has to help. And to make everyone want to help, some of it has got to be fun.

Recycling is a good example. Some people think of it as a chore. Other people think it's fun. We like to separate glass by color, crush and rattle the cans together, bundle up newspapers, and haul the stuff out to get recycled. Part of the fun is making play out of a chore. The rest of the fun is the satisfaction of doing something good for the planet.

By now you've heard all about serious things like air pollution and rainforest destruction. Those lessons are important and have a place in our lives — but so does fun! So use this book to make your own games. These games can be as fun as any store-bought game and will not hurt the environment!

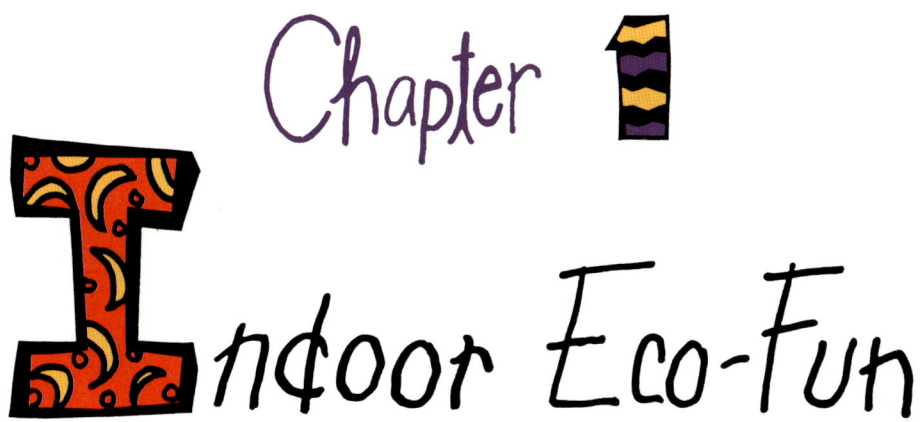

Chapter 1
Indoor Eco-Fun

ECO-JIGSAW PUZZLE

Pick up the pieces of the Earth! Make an eco-jigsaw puzzle.

- A magazine with colorful pictures in it. The pictures can be of oceans, forests, mountains, animals, or anything you like. The bigger the picture the better.

- A piece of cardboard or posterboard as large as the picture

- White glue

- Scissors

Instructions for Eco-Jigsaw Puzzle:

Step 1 Cut the picture from the magazine.

Step 2 Cut the posterboard or cardboard to the same size as the picture.

Step 3 Spread an even layer of glue across the entire surface of the cardboard.

Step 4 Stick the picture down onto the cardboard and smooth it so that the picture is glued evenly and securely.

Step 5 Let the picture dry overnight.

Step 6 With the scissors CAREFULLY cut the cardboard out into different shapes. Look at a store-bought jigsaw puzzle to give you an idea of what kind of shapes to cut.

Step 7 Once the jigsaw puzzle is cut up, you can put it back together again to re-make the picture. The more complicated the cuts, the harder it will be to assemble it. Trade puzzles with your friends.

20 QUESTIONS ECO-BOARD GAME

A board game that won't make you bored!

- Objects such as pennies, thimbles, and small toys to use as game pieces

- Pencils, pens, crayons, and /or magic markers

- A sheet of posterboard or cardboard
- Old magazines

- A package of small index cards
- Scratch paper

- A ruler and a yardstick
- Scissors

- White glue and tape
- Dice

Instructions for 20 Questions Eco-Board Game:

Step 1 Draw a path on the game board that the players will follow. Use magic markers, pencils, and crayons. Make at least thirty spaces on the board. Some spaces could say "lose a turn" or "advance two spaces."

Step 2 Decorate the ag,me board with pictures relating to ecology. Use pictures from old magazines, cut them out, glue them down.

Step 3 Write down 20 to 50 questions about ecology on index cards. Write the answers below them. Use questions from the Eco-Quiz on page 13 for examples. Make up your own questions using text books, encyclopedias and magazines. If you don't want to know the answers in advance, ask someone who isn't playing to write down questions.

Step 4 Put some wild cards in with the index cards. Wild cards could say things like, "Oil spill - go back three spaces," or "You saved a tree - go forward two spaces."

Step 5 Shuffle the index cards and lay them face-down on the game board.

Step 6 Each player takes a turn by rolling the dice.

Step 7 Another player takes the top card off the pile of eco-questions and asks the person whose turn it is the question. If the answer is correct, the player advances the number of spaces on the dice.

Step 8 Whoever reaches the end first wins.

ECO-CARDS

The Six of Mountains! The King of Pandas! The Ace of Smoke-stacks! Make your own Eco-Cards!

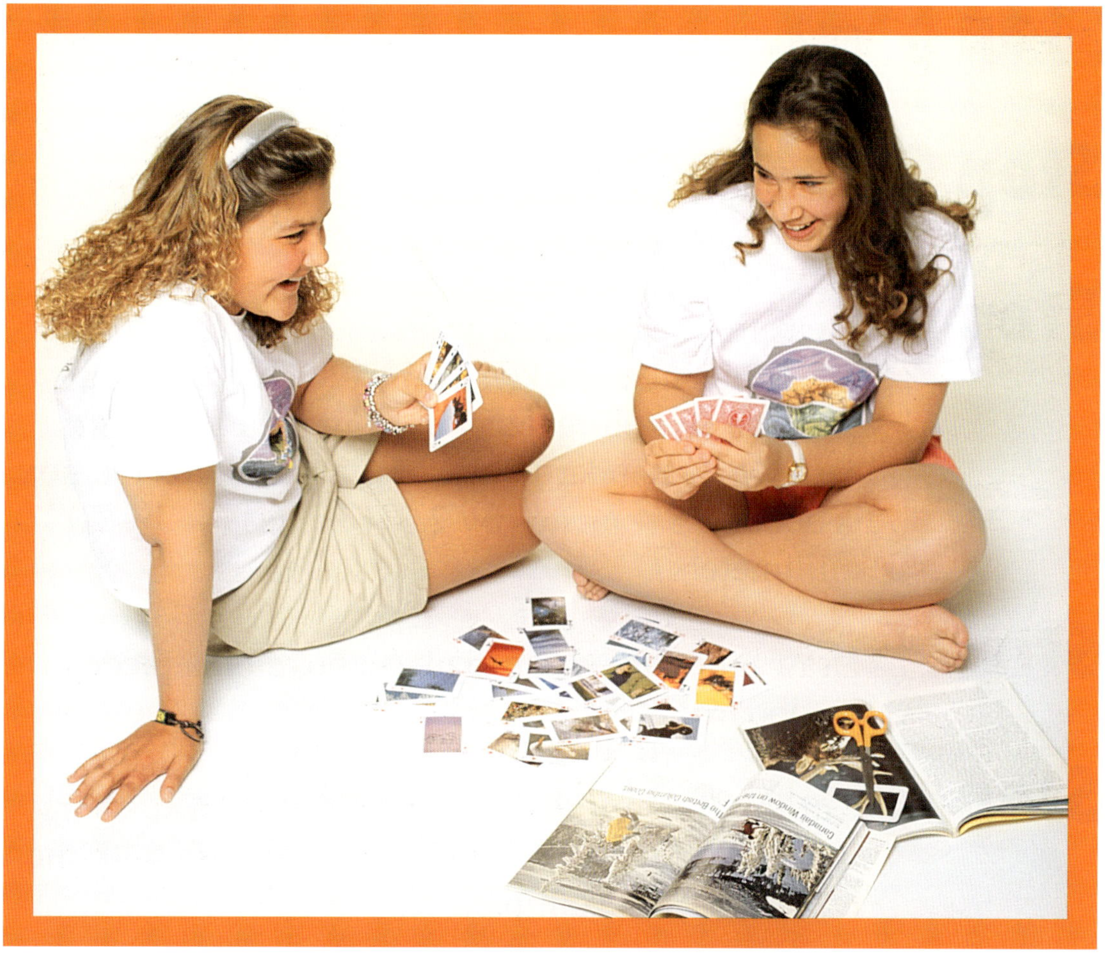

You will need these items

- an old deck of playing cards
- old magazines that contain many pictures
- a piece of cardboard the size of the playing cards or bigger
- a ruler
- scissors
- glue

Instructions for Eco-Cards:

First make a picture frame:

Step 1 Find a king, queen, or jack in the deck of playing cards.

Step 2 The picture of the king, queen, or jack should be framed in a box on the card. See example.

Step 3 Measure the box that holds the picture of the king, queen, or jack. This box should be about 3/8 inch (9 millimeters) in from the edge of the card. On a standard deck of playing cards the box is about 1 3/4 inches by 2 3/4 inches (44 by 70 millimeters).

Step 4 Draw a box the same size as above on a piece of cardboard.

Step 5 Cut the box out of the cardboard with scissors. Recycle the box and save the cardboard with the hole in it. See example.

Step 6 You now have a stencil that you can lay on magazine pictures.

To make the cards:

Step 1 Make each suit of cards an environmental theme. In this example we will use air for clubs, Earth for spades, water for diamonds, and animals for hearts.

Step 2 Find thirteen pictures in magazines that are of the four different subjects. The pictures need be only as big as a playing card. Air pictures may include clouds, sky, storms, rainbows, smokestacks, etc. Water pictures may be mountains, trees, cities, rocks, landfills, etc. Animal pictures may be pictures of any animals including humans.

Step 3 Lay your picture frame on the pictures you selected.

Step 4 Trace the edges of your picture frame with a light pencil or marker.

Step 5 Cut out the picture along the trace lines.

Step 6 Glue the pictures to the center of the playing cards. Use enough glue so that the pictures are secure. Be sure to leave the numbers showing.

Step 7 Glue all air pictures to clubs. Glue all Earth pictures to spades. Glue all water pictures to diamonds. Glue all animal pictures to hearts.

Step 8 Lay all the cards down in an out-of-the-way place and let them dry overnight. Do not stack the cards or they will stick together! Lay them out one by one.

Step 9 The cards may not shuffle as smoothly with pictures glued to them. Shuffle them by mixing them up on the floor or table top.

Step 10 Play card games with your eco-cards. The king of air beats the four of fish!

ECO-QUIZ

Have fun testing your knowledge of issues concerning the environment.

Answer the following questions. Write your answers on a separate sheet of paper. DO NOT MARK THE BOOK! The correct answers are on page 30.

1 If all the styrofoam cups made in one day were laid end to end, they would stretch:

   a. Across New York City

   b. Around the world

   c. Across Canada

2 How much of the Earth's water can humans use for drinking water?

   a. All of it

   b. Half of it

   c. Only one percent

3 Solar energy comes from the sun. If collected in solar collectors, how much heat does the sun provide every day?

   a. Enough to cook breakfast for every schoolkid in North America

   b. Enough to give suntans to every move star in the world

   c. Enough to heat every home in the world for one year

4 One way to help save the rainforest is to:

   a. Eat candy

   b. Play outside on a rainy day

   c. Take a monkey to lunch

5 Americans throw away 2.5 million plastic bottles every:

   a. Year

   b. Hour

   c. Now and then

6 What uses the most water in your house?

   a. The kitchen sink

   b. Your goldfish

   c. Your toilet

7 Which of these items is considered litter?

a. Cigarette butts

b. Soda cans

c. Apple cores

8 It takes one 15-year-old tree to make only 700 paper bags. Many grocery stores use that many paper bags in:

a. One month

b. One hour

c. One year

9 If all the trash produced in one day in America were piled up in one place it would fill:

a. Your bedroom to the ceiling (but no one would notice)

b. A domed football stadium — twice

c. Your school's gymnasium

10 The best way kids can help save the Earth is to:

a. Recycle paper, glass, plastic, and aluminum

b. Join environmental organizations

c. Learn as much as they can about the environment

(Answers to the Eco-Quiz on page 30)

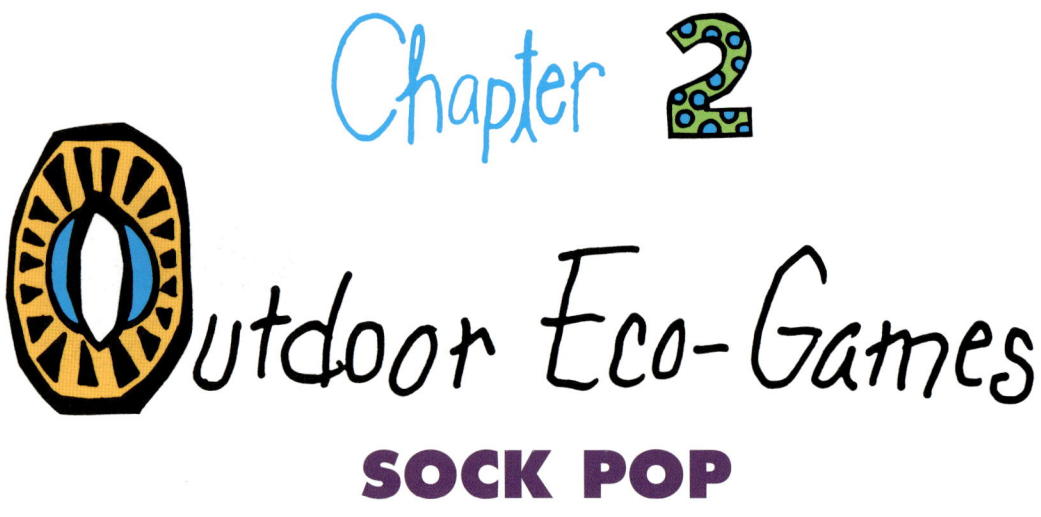
Chapter 2
Outdoor Eco-Games

SOCK POP

Too many old socks in your drawer? Recycle yours into a toy for all seasons.

You will need these items

- A clean old sock. A longer sock works best.
- A rubber ball or tennis ball.

Instructions for Sock Pop:

Step 1 Put a tennis ball or rubber ball into a sock.

Step 2 Tie a knot in the sock just above the ball.

Step 3 To throw the sock pop, grab the end opposite of the tennis ball and whirl it around a few times.

Step 4 You can play catch with the sock pop or have throwing contests. Be careful, the sock pop really flies.

Throwing the Sock Pop.

SLIPPIN' AND SLIDIN'

Use a garden hose to turn a sheet of old plastic into fun on a hot summer's day.

You will need these items

- An old sheet of plastic from 8 to 20 feet (2.4 to 6 meters) long. You can use an old plastic drop cloth, ground cloth or tarp. Make sure the plastic isn't too dirty or covered with paint.

- A garden hose and an outdoor faucet

- A garden sprinkler (optional)

Instructions for Slippin' and Slidin'

Step 1 Find an open area to lay the plastic on the ground. Hills are a great place.

Step 2 Spray the plastic with water. If you have a garden sprinkler, put it at the top of the sheet spraying a light stream of water on the plastic. Try not to waste water. Only use enough to keep the plastic wet.

Step 3 Get a running start.

Step 4 When you reach the plastic, slide!

DO THE CAN CAN

Make stilts from recycled materials!

- Two large clean juice cans
- A punch-type can opener
- Masking tape
- Scissors
- About ten feet of rope

Instructions for making Can Stilts

Step 1 Use the can opener to punch two holes in the sides of the cans. Punch the holes near the bottom of the cans on opposite sides from each other. The punched holes should be made on the other side of the open ends of the cans.

Step 2 Carefully tape the sharp edges with masking tape.

Step 3 Loop about five feet of rope through the holes in each can.

Step 4 Stand on the cans and hold the rope in your hands.

Step 5 Knot the rope where you can hold it tight while walking on the can stilts.

Step 6 Walk on your stilts and listen to them clomp.

ECO-SCAVENGER HUNT

The first person to collect all the things on the list wins!

- Paper
- Pencil or pen

Directions for Eco-Scavenger Hunt:

1 Use a pencil and paper to copy any or all of the item from the list below. Try to use items that are hard to find but are still available where you are playing. Each person playin should receive an exact copy of the list.

2 Each person must find all the items on the list.

3 The first person who brings all the items on the list back to home base wins.

4 Form teams with several people hunting form items on one list.

5 Make your own list of items to be found.

6 IMPORTANT: Do not walk into people's yards and take things for your scavenger hunt. Only list items that are available where you are playing in parks, playgrounds, or your own yard.

21

ECO-SCAVENGER HUNT LIST:

- A maple leaf
- An oak leaf
- A dandelion
- A red flower
- A piece of litter
- A plastic six-pack ring
- Something made of aluminum
- Something made from recycled paper
- A styrofoam cup or container
- A paper bag
- A plastic bag
- A shell
- A plant seed
- An apple
- A pink flower
- An acorn
- A pine cone
- A crooked twig
- Something purple
- A red rock
- A clover
- Something in the shape of a triangle
- Something (fill in the color)
- Something (fill in the shape)

You get the idea. Try not to make the list too long, too short, too hard, or too easy. When you're done playing, recycle the trash.

Chapter 3

Serious Fun
THE GARBAGE GAME

The United States generates about 160 million tons (144 billion kilograms) of garbage every year. That's enough trash to fill 63,000 garbage trucks every day! To solve this rubbish problem we must reduce the amount of garbage we produce. And we must recycle everything we can.

Most people aren't aware of how much garbage their family produces. They just take it out to the trashcan when their garbage pail is full. But if we knew how much garbage we were throwing away, we might change our shopping habits. By playing the Garbage Game, we can find out everything we've wanted to know about our garbage. Then we can find ways to reduce, reuse, and recycle.

Instructions for the Garbage Game:

Step 1 — Make several copies of the chart below.

Step 2 — Each time your family brings home items form the store, fill out the chart. Look at what has been bought and see how much of it is packaging that will be thrown away. For instance, if you by a twelve-pack of soft drinks, you will have 12 aluminum cans and one cardboard box. If you buy a toy, you will have plastic wrapping and the cardboard box that it came in. If you're not sure what the packaging is made of, ask someone to help you.

Step 3 — Keep track of all your family's garbage for one week.

Step 4 — After one week, using a calculator, multiply the garbage numbers by 52. This will tell you about how much garbage your family makes in 52 weeks, or one year.

Step 5 — Try a class project where everybody in your class plays the garbage game. Add all the numbers together and see how much garbage your class makes.

Step 6 — Look up "Recycling" in your telephone book and find out how you can start a recycling program for your family.

Step 7

If your family already recycles, find out how much trash isn't recycled. Try to find ways to reduce your family's waste.

Copy this chart — Do not write in book!

Waste items	Total number	Will it be recycled?
aluminum cans		
aluminum foil		
cardboard boxes		
glass bottles and jars		
magazines		
newspapers		
paper bags		
plastic bags		
plastic bottles		
plastic containers		
styrofoam containers		
other		

ADOPT A PARK

Make a difference! Adopt a park, lake, forest, or stream.

Is there a park, playground, or recreational area in your neighborhood that needs some tender loving care? Parks need people like you to help them regain their beauty. Organize your friends and classmates to adopt a park.

How to adopt a park:

Step 1 Find a park in your neighborhood that needs attention. If there is no park, is there a play ground, river bank, or lake?

Step 2 Visit the park with a notebook and pencil. Write down what improvements the park needs. Is it littered with trash? Are there broken fences or equipment? Do weeds need to be trimmed? Are there enough trash cans? Is pollution being dumped nearby? Write down whatever problems you see. Later you can use the list to get things fixed.

Step 3 Almost every park could use a good cleaning. Organize a group of friends or your class at school to clean up the park on a Saturday afternoon.

Step 4 Get parents involved! It's their park too!

Step 1 Write a letter to the local newspaper explaining what improvements the park needs.

27

Step 2 Call the mayor or city hall and explain what improvements the park needs.

Step 3 Call the local newspaper or television stations and tell them why you and your friends are planning to adopt the park. Tell reporters the problems you found in the park. A story in the newspaper or on television will help your cause.

Step 4 Try to get permission to make further improvements such as planting trees or painting fences. This is something the local government must approve.

Step 5 Write your congressional representative and tell him or her about problems with your park. You can also write your city councilperson and state congressional representative. Their addresses are listed in the telephone directory and available at the library.

Step 6 Good luck!

Target Earth™ kids.

Answers to Eco-Quiz

1. The answer is b. Believe it or not, if all the styrofoam cups made in one day were laid end to end, they would stretch around the entire planet — and then some.

2. The answer is c. Of all the water on Earth, 97% is salt water that is undrinkable by humans. Only 3% of the Earth's water is fresh water. Of that only 1% is available for use by humans.

3. The answer is c. The Earth receives enough solar energy every day — free — to heat every home in the world for one year. Unfortunately, most homes are heated by wood, coal, oil, gas, or nuclear generated electricity. All those energy sources have negative environmental impacts.

4. The answer is a. Here's a chance to eat candy and do some good. Products like Rainforest Crunch candy use 150,000 pounds (67,5000 kilograms) of nuts grown in the rainforest every year. The profits from the candy are used to protect the rainforest. By using renewable products from the rain forest, we help support its survival. When people can make a living harvesting fruit and nuts from the rainforest, they're less likely to cut the trees down for lumber. Buy fruit and nuts that come from the rainforest. Have a snack — save a tree.

5. The answer is b. It's sad but true, Americans throw away 2.5 million plastic bottles every hour! Recycle plastic or buy products in glass or aluminum containers. Then recycle them.

6. The answer is c. The toilet uses an average of 40% of the water used in a home. The water we use in our toilets starts out as fresh drinking water. Americans use 450 billion gallons (1.7 trillion liters) of fresh water every day! Put a plastic jug filled with water in the back of your toilet and save an average of 5,000 gallons (19,000 liters) of fresh water a year.

7. The answers are a, b, and c. Almost anything that gets thrown on the ground and is left there is considered litter. It makes the Earth look like a garbage can. And litter is harmful to animals. Cigarettes cause cancer and their butts take almost a year to disappear; soda cans take more than 200 years! Apple cores lying next to the highway often attract animals who later might be hit by cars.

8. Large grocery stores use at least 700 paper bags an hour. Multiply that times all the grocery stores in the country. Thousands of trees a day are cut down and made into paper bags. Use a cloth bag at the store or don't use any bag at all. Recycle all paper bags.

9. The answer is b. Americans produce 154 million tons (140 billion kilograms) of garbage every day. That's enough to fill the New Orleans Superdome from top to bottom twice a day, every day. Half of this trash could be recycled.

10. All of them! You can make a difference!

Connect With Books

Burnie, David. *How Nature Works*. London: Dorling Kindersley Ltd., 1991.

Buzzworm Magazine. *1992 Earth Journal*. Boulder, Colorado: Buzzworm Books, 1992.

Earth Works Group. *50 Simple Things Kids Can Do to Save the Earth.* Kansas City, New York: Andrews and McMeel, 1990.

Earth Works Group. *50 Simple Things You Can Do to Save the Earth.* Berkeley, California: Earthworks Press, 1989.

Editors of Owl and Chickadee Magazine. *Outdoor Fun.* Boston: Little Brown & Company, 1989.

Fluegelman, Andrew. *New Games.* New York: Doubleday, 1981.

Hamilton, Leslie. *Child's Play 6-12.* New York: Crown Publishers, 1991.

Lamb, Marjorie. *2 Minutes a Day for a Greener Planet.* San Francisco: Harper & Row, 1990.

MacEachern, Diane. *Save Our Planet.* New York: Dell Publishing, 1990.

Schwartz, Linda. *Earth Book for Kids.* Santa Barbara, California: The Learning Works, Inc., 1990.

Target Earth™ Commitment

At Target, we're committed to the environment. We show this commitment not only through our own internal efforts but also through the programs we sponsor in the communities where we do business.

Our commitment to children and the environment began when we became the Founding International Sponsor for Kids for Saving Earth, a non-profit environmental organization for kids. We helped launch the program in 1989 and supported its growth to three-quarters of a million club members in just three years.

Our commitment to children's environmental education led to the development of an environmental curriculum called Target Earth™, aimed at getting kids involved in their education and in their world.

In addition, we worked with Abdo & Daughters Publishing to develop the Target Earth™ Earthmobile, an environmental science library on wheels that can be used in libraries, or rolled from classroom to classroom.

Target believes that the children are our future and the future of our planet. Through education, they will save the world!

Minneapolis-based Target Stores is an upscale discount department store chain of 517 stores in 33 states coast-to-coast, and is the largest division of Dayton Hudson Corporation, one of the nation's leading retailers.